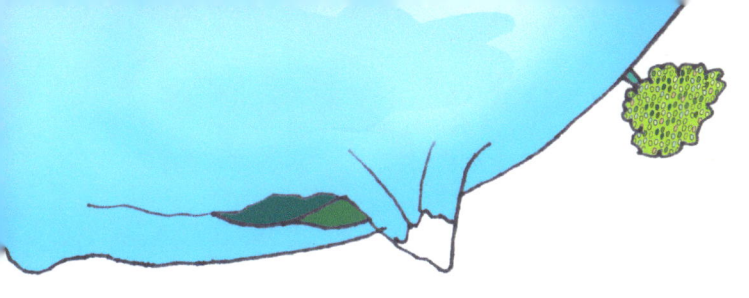

*To Kartik, Dudhaa
and my grandparents.*

Copyright © 2017 by Sanaya Kondaskar OTR Kathy Colunga OTR
Cover and illustrations by Charity Russell

All rights reserved. No part of this book may be reproduced in any form by any electronicor mechanical means, including photocopying, recording, or information storage and retrieval without written permission from the author.

PLANET L

JIMMY AND THE MAGNASAURS

written by
Sanaya Kondaskar
Kathy Colunga

illustrated by
Charity Russell

"Jimmy, get your homework done!
I don't want to tell you again and again",
yelled Jimmy's mom from the kitchen.
Jimmy hated doing his homework.
Homework meant coming face to face
with his biggest enemies - letters.
He could never remember them!

Jimmy didn't even bother about what his mom was saying and instead went down into the basement to play.

Jimmy was busy playing with his ball when suddenly it hit an old book on the floor. He had never seen such a big mystical book before.

The book was heavy and covered in dust. He wiped away the dust with his hands and began to read the name of the book. "PLANET L"

'What in the world..." he thought.

Curious, he flipped through the pages. Bright ribbons of light started streaming out of the pages and pulled him inside the book.

Jimmy opened his eyes and saw that he was in an old cave with two doors in front of him. They had strange symbols. A voice startled him; it seemed to come from everywhere. "Jimmy, my boy! Welcome to Planet L, the most literate planet in the Boombastic Galaxy! and the land where the letters live!

You were brave to open the book of Planet L and looks like you hate doing your homework. The old wise book was in search for someone like you for a long time. The book chose you, Jimmy!"

The voice continued, "You are here for a mission. You see those doors? You must enter the world of Planet L through these doors and complete two missions. If you succeed, you will go home and letters will be your friends for life and writing will be fun again. But if you do not succeed with the mission, you will never be able to go home..."

Jimmy walked towards the first door that had a dinosaur symbol on it. He pushed it open and entered the strange world of Planet L.

What a wonderful sight! The pebbles were glowing, the birds made funny sounds and the trees had glowing fruits, cupcakes and candies hanging high on their branches. It was magical!

Suddenly he heard someone crying.. 'boo boo'.

He turned around to find five small dinosaurs crying. They were tiny and all looked the same.

"You must be Jimmy from planet Earth! Your mission is to help us become big and tall again" said one of the dinosaur.

"How do I help you? I want to complete the missions and go back home."

The dinosaurs climbed on top of each other and made a dinosaur ladder. "Climb up Jimmy", said one of the dinosaurs, "and get us the glowing fruit. We always fall short of one creature!"

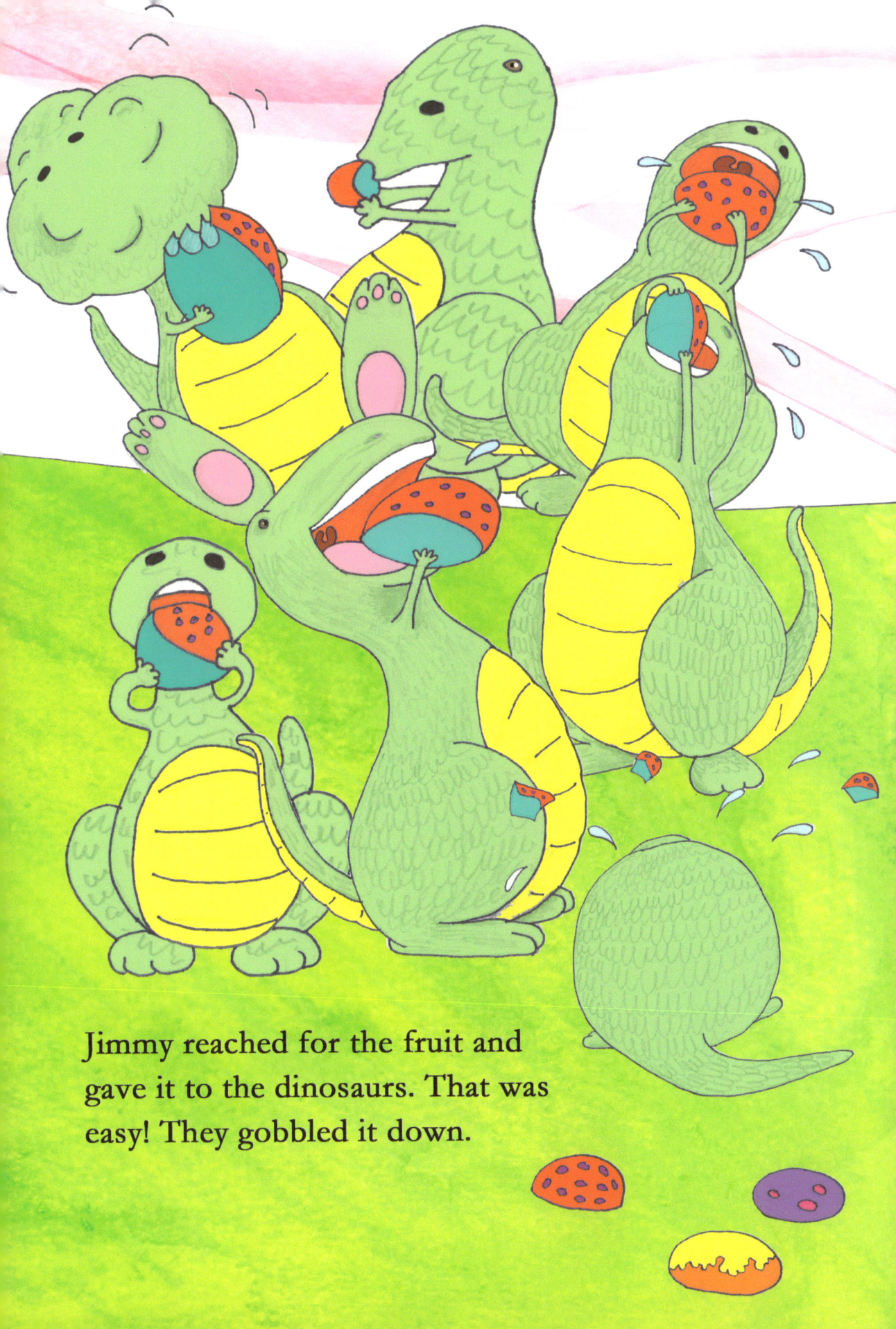

Jimmy reached for the fruit and gave it to the dinosaurs. That was easy! They gobbled it down.

Suddenly, they all changed shape and grew as tall as the sky. They all looked different and reminded Jimmy of the letters he so hated. One dinosaur changed into a shape of letter "t" with a big purple bow tie. "I am **t-saurus**. I love drinking tea and eating sandwiches", it said to Jimmy's amazement.

Another one grew soo tall and lean, similar to the letter "l". It looked down at Jimmy and sang, "I am **l-saurus**, the leanest and longest of them all. I like to run, jump, skip, hop and sing songs all day long."

Then Jimmy gazed up at two eyes looking down from the sky. "I am **f-sauras**. As a child I got my head stuck in a cookie jar and nothing could get me out. They pulled and tugged and spun me around until my neck became so tall that it hit the sky! Now I keep it bent like a cane so I can see the ground", it said.

Jimmy could not believe what he was seeing! Over walked another dinosaur that looked like the letter "b".
"I am **b-saurus** with a big belly. I like to eat candy and cupcakes and all the sweet treats. Will you join me Jimmy?" it asked while his belly was shaking with laughter.

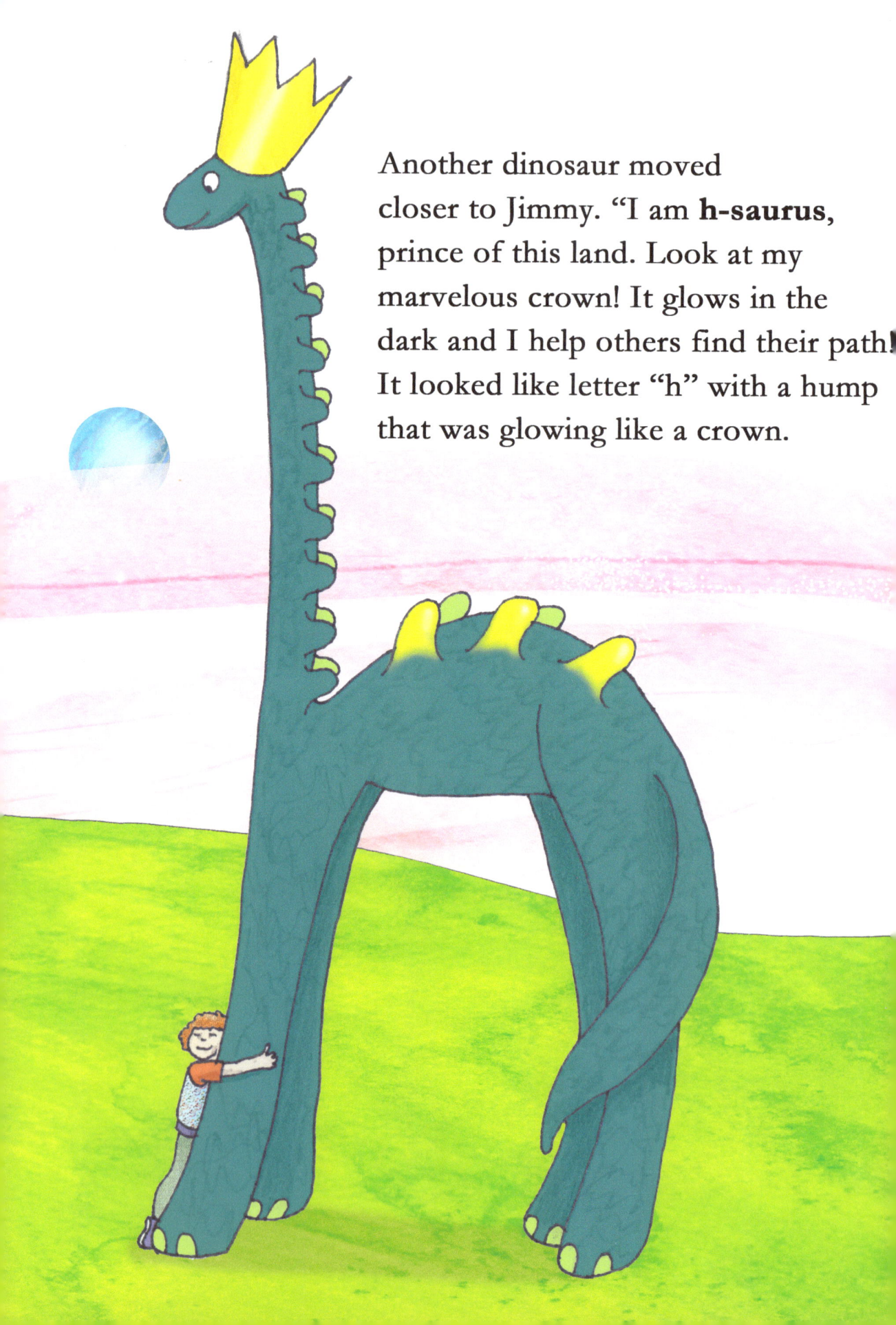

Another dinosaur moved closer to Jimmy. "I am **h-saurus**, prince of this land. Look at my marvelous crown! It glows in the dark and I help others find their path! It looked like letter "h" with a hump that was glowing like a crown.

Then another dinosaur stepped over and announced, "I am **k-sauras**. I like to do karate and judo. I spend my time kicking in the arena. Ahh! I am glad my legs are finally big and strong again."

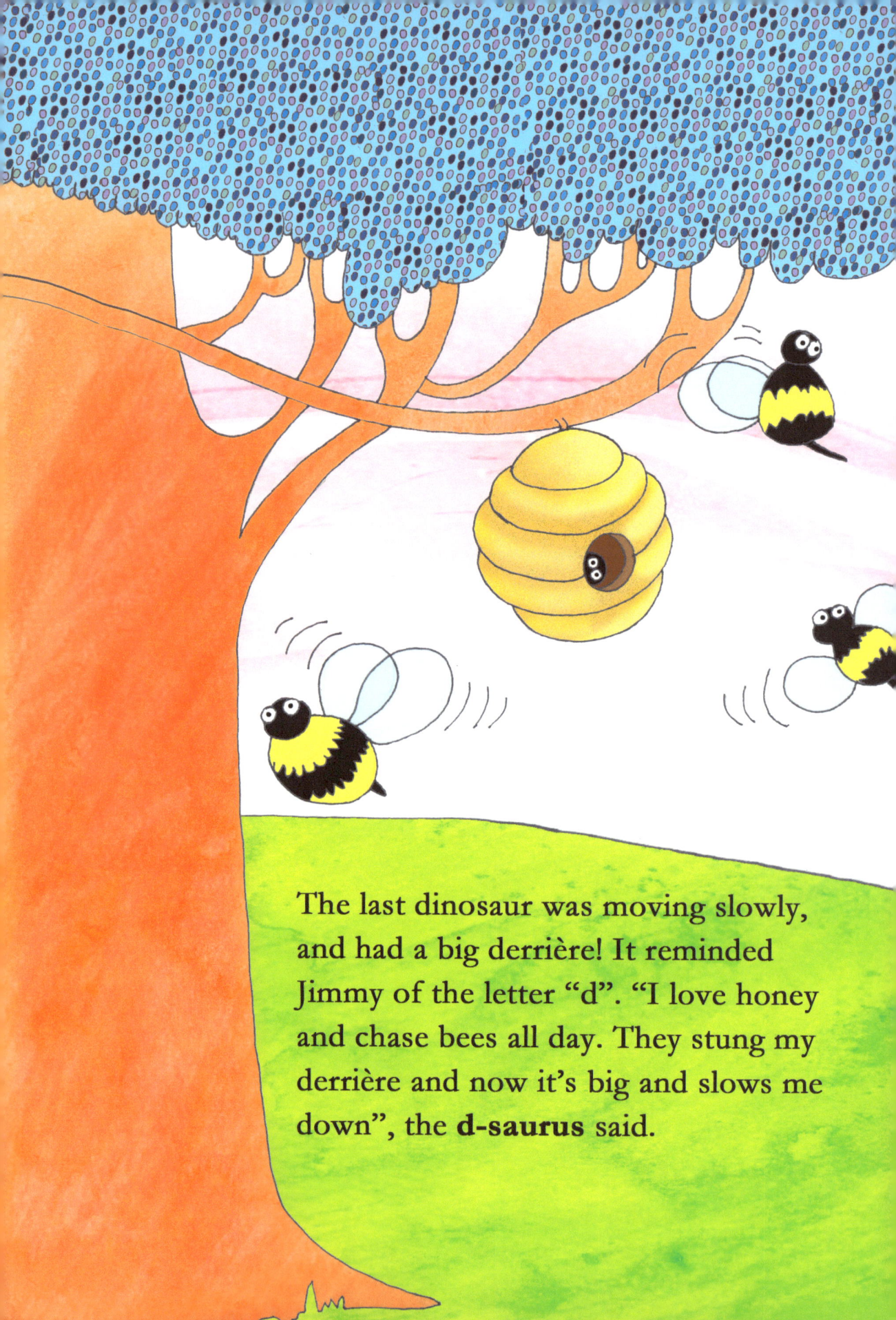

The last dinosaur was moving slowly, and had a big derrière! It reminded Jimmy of the letter "d". "I love honey and chase bees all day. They stung my derrière and now it's big and slows me down", the **d-saurus** said.

"Together we are the **Magnasaurs** of Planet L." The dinosaurs all gathered around Jimmy and started telling Jimmy stories of all their adventures. They also had a big magnificent Magnasaurs party!

Jimmy enjoyed their company, "Thank you Magnasaurs! You all look like letters in the English alphabet and I will never forget you! Now I bet homework will become very easy and my handwriting much better."

They said good bye and led Jimmy towards another door. It had a strange masked figure on it. "What in the world...", said Jimmy as he opened the second door...

www.ingramcontent.com/pod-product-compliance
Lightning Source LLC
LaVergne TN
LVHW071029070426
835507LV00002B/81